WILDLIFE
AROUND US

FIELD GUIDE & DRAWING BOOK: VOLUME 1

Learn to identify and draw birds, insects,
and other wildlife from the great outdoors!

Quarto is the authority on a wide range of topics.
Quarto educates, entertains, and enriches the lives of our readers—
enthusiasts and lovers of hands-on living.
www.quartoknows.com

The National Wildlife Federation & Ranger Rick contributors: Children's Publication Staff, Licensing
Staff, and in-house naturalist David Mizejewski.
© National Wildlife Federation. All rights reserved.
www.RangerRick.com

Illustrations by Diana Fisher. Photos © Shutterstock, except Anna's hummingbird photo on page 16
© Charles Gonzales.

6 Orchard Road, Suite 100
Lake Forest, CA 92630
quartoknows.com
Visit our blogs at quartoknows.com

Printed in China
1 3 5 7 9 10 8 6 4 2

TABLE OF CONTENTS

Blue Jay

Welcome to Ranger Rick's field guide to North American critters! Join us as you learn about the insects, birds, reptiles, and amphibians that surround you, from the Pacific tree frog and monarch butterfly to the bald eagle. This book contains 26 step-by-step drawing projects to help you bring each featured animal to life. You'll also find fieldwork tips, fascinating animal facts, and colorful photographs throughout to inspire you in your quest for knowledge. Enjoy the journey!

North America has a diverse landscape, from deserts and grasslands to mountains and even tropical areas. No matter where you live, Ranger Rick and this handy field guide will help you discover the animals around you.

GETTING STARTED

In this chapter, you'll learn how to prepare for outdoor excursions—from packing your backpack and taking great photos to recording notes and drawings.

When we're busy at school and in our homes, it can be hard to remember that people are part of nature! We are animals, too—and we're an important part of the circle of life. Unlike other animals, we have the unique ability to study and protect other species. The first step in accomplishing this is to get outside and learn about nature. Let's start NOW!

Why spend time outdoors?

You'll get smarter.
The world around you is fascinating, with living organisms everywhere you look! The more time you spend outdoors, the more you'll notice, be curious, and learn.

You'll help animals.
The more you learn about the animals that surround us, the more likely you'll be to protect them. Human decisions can have a big impact on the natural environment, so you will use your new knowledge to conserve threatened animals and the plants they need to thrive.

You'll be healthier.
Fresh air, sun, and exercise make exploring the outdoors great for your body. It improves distance vision too! Spending time in nature is also proven to calm your mind and lift your spirits.

NATURALIST FIELDWORK

A *naturalist* is someone who studies natural life, like plants and animals. And *fieldwork* is what people do when they go out into the real world, into nature, to study, rather than learning in a classroom or lab. Once you get outside and start observing nature, you will be a naturalist doing fieldwork! Naturalists who go into the field prepared are the ones who do the best work and have the most fun.

Bring:

A backpack with the following:	
	Bottle of water
	Pencil
	Notebook for sketching and taking notes
	Magnifying glass (for viewing small critters)
	Binoculars
	Camera
	Map or GPS device and compass

Wear:

	Hat
	Sunscreen
	Socks and comfortable, sturdy shoes
	Appropriate clothing for the weather

Be:

1

Quiet and still. You can't observe critters if you've scared them away!

2

At a distance. You don't want to hurt any animals or get hurt yourself! You could get bitten or stung, so keep a safe distance.

3

Patient. The longer you watch, the more you'll learn. It can take a long time to spot a creature, so practice patience.

Go with:

A research assistant. Your assistant is there to help you observe and record, and also for safety. If you venture outside of your backyard, make sure your assistant is an adult.

CAMERAS & BINOCULARS

You can see up-close details of an insect through a magnifying glass, but how can you view more detail or an animal that's far away from you? With a camera or binoculars! Here are some tips for using cameras and binoculars.

To get the best pictures:

Use the "optical zoom" instead of "digital zoom," and set your camera to take the largest photos that it possibly can. (You or an adult may need to read the camera's user manual to find out how to do this.)

Use good lighting. Color and detail will disappear into dark shadows if your subject has the sun behind it. Shoot with the sun behind you, if possible, or to the side of your subject.

Stay as still as possible to cut down on blurry pictures. Hold your elbows against your sides and breathe out before snapping the photo. Or prop your camera on something (such as a rock or log) to steady it.

Take a lot of pictures. You'll get a lot of blurry ones, especially when the animals are moving, but you're bound to also get a few really good ones!

Using binoculars:

When using binoculars, first look at something near the animal that won't fly or run away, like a tree branch or a chimney on top of a house. Then bring the binoculars up to your eyes, find what you were looking at, and then slowly look around for the animal.

Diopter: Some binoculars have a "diopter," usually on the right eye, which allows you to adjust the focus even more.

Central Focus Wheel: Turn this wheel until you can see as clearly as possible.

Neck Strap: The neck strap keeps you from dropping your binoculars and allows you to grab them in a split second if you see something.

SKETCHING & COLORING ANIMALS

To draw the animals in this book, you'll need a few art supplies: paper or a sketchbook, a pencil, an eraser, and a pencil sharpener. Then find some coloring tools, such as crayons, colored pencils, or markers. You'll need an array of bright, beautiful colors for the animals in this book!

Many naturalists are also artists! They spend time observing and recording all the visual details of their subjects. Many of them use paint, such as watercolor, to add color to their work. Watercolor is one of the easiest paints to use—you can clean it up with soap and water! Tempera and acrylic are good non-toxic options, too.

Go outside and try to find the animals in this book (check out the maps provided with each animal to know if it can be found in your area), and keep your eye out for other creatures, too. Observe each critter and see what makes it unique. You can try sketching outside (don't forget to bring a sketchbook, a pencil, and an eraser!), you can take a photograph for reference to use when drawing later, and you can use this book for easy step-by-step drawing instructions.

The step-by-step instructions in this book start with basic shapes, such as circles, triangles, and rectangles. Follow the steps in order, copying the new lines in each step and erasing when necessary. Before you know it, you'll have a complete sketch to color! You can use colored pencils, crayons, markers, or even paints to bring these animals to life.

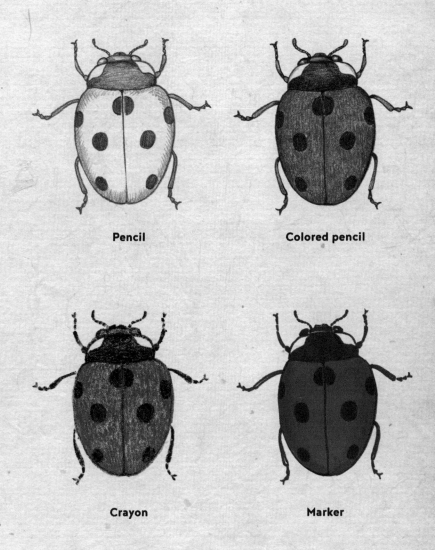

Pencil

Colored pencil

Crayon

Marker

YOUR NATURALIST NOTEBOOK

Now that you're all packed and ready to do some fieldwork, know that there's no right or wrong way to fill up your naturalist notebook. Just observe and record!

See a bird in a tree? Watch it and record everything you see and hear. What does it look like? What is its main color? Are there any other colors? How big is it? What is its shape like? What shape is its beak—long and thin, short and stocky, really big compared to its head?

What is the bird doing? Is it eating something? How does it move around? Is it preening its feathers? Is it making any kind of noise?

American Goldfinch
- Type: Bird
- Season seen: Spring
- Date seen: May 3
- Size: About 3" long

Found American goldfinch while on a family hike in Washington.

Small bird with a short, pointed beak.

Yellow feathers with black markings on face, wings, and tail.

Repeats high-pitched chirps and twitters.

Moves very quickly from branch to branch! Hard to track.

Many new species are discovered every year—and about half of all newly discovered species are insects. Maybe you could find something new while doing fieldwork!

So get outside, look for critters, and have fun!

Using This Field Guide:

Discover interesting bits of information about the featured animal.

Follow the steps to draw each animal on a sheet of paper or in your own sketchbook.

Familiarize yourself with each animal through photographs.

Learn the scientific name, diet, size, and locations of each animal.

AMAZING BIRDS

Ornithology is the study of birds. When you're watching and recording information about birds, you are a naturalist and an ornithologist in training!

Northern cardinal male (left) and female (right)

Anna's hummingbird

John James Audubon is one of the most famous birdwatchers in history. He was an ornithologist, a naturalist, and an artist. He studied and painted all types of American birds in the 1800s, and prints of his paintings sell for thousands of dollars at auctions today. Audubon also identified 25 new species and has many conservation groups named after him. Wow!

Birdwatching Tips

Know your birds.

Get a book or pocket field guide that tells you what birds can be found in your area. These guides show you what the birds look like, where to find them (high up in trees, feeding on the ground, swimming in the water), and how they behave.

Know their calls.

Use the Internet to look up recordings of bird songs and calls. You can hear many birds before you can see them. If you recognize a bird sound, then you can look around and try to spot it!

Use binoculars.

With binoculars, you will be able to see a lot of up-close detail of birds (at least when they're sitting still!) that you might not ever see with your naked eye.

House Finch

Offer treats.

If you want to observe birds from the comfort of your own home, place a bird feeder or tray of birdseed near a window, and watch birds from inside.

IDENTIFYING BIRDS

Size

Compare an unfamiliar bird with one you know well. Is it smaller than a sparrow? Tall like a stork? Bigger than a robin?

Shape

What is the bird's overall shape? What type of bill does it have? Is the tail long or short? Is there a crest on the head? Do you see a long neck or long legs?

Color

What is the bird's main color? What other colors are present?

Song Sparrow

Size & Shape: Small. Bulky, short bill, round head, long and round tail.

Color: Brown and light gray with streaks on its chest.

Wood Stork

Size & Shape: Very large. Long legs, long and thick bill that curves downward.

Color: Mostly white with black on the wings and tail.

American Robin

Size & Shape: Medium to large. Round body with fairly long legs and tail.

Color: Dark gray and orange.

Habitat & Behavior

Think about where you are, what kind of habitat you're in, and what season it is. For example, if you're on the East Coast, the bird you see is probably not a western meadowlark. If there's no water around, it's probably not a kingfisher. And, of course, you're much more likely to see common birds than rare ones.

What is the bird doing? Is it looking for food in a tree, on the ground, or in water? Does it perch on a tree branch or cling to the trunk?

Is it making a noise? You can ID birds by ear, too. Each species has a sound of its own.

Song Sparrow

Habitat: Seen year-round in much of the United States; winters in the South and breeds in the north and Canada.

Behavior: Forages for insects on the ground but finds a low perch to sing from. Short, loud song at varying rhythms.

American Robin

Habitat: Seen year-round in most of the United States.

Behavior: Forages on the ground for earthworms and insects. Also found in trees and shrubs feeding on berries and fruits.

Wood Stork

Habitat: Found year-round in marshy habitats in southern Florida and in winter on the southern coast.

Behavior: Wades in marshes with its bill in the water to find food. Usually silent.

BALD EAGLE

Haliaeetus leucocephalus

The bald eagle has piercing yellow eyes, a head covered in white feathers (juveniles' heads are brown), and an impressive wingspan of more than 6 feet!

The bald eagle is part of a group of birds called "sea eagles," which is known for diets heavy in fish.

The bald eagle is both a scavenger and a skilled hunter that uses its powerful talons to pluck fish from the water.

Order: Accipitriformes
Family: Accipitridae

Diet: Fish, birds, snakes, crabs, small mammals, and carrion

Size: 43 inches long, up to 14 pounds

Habitat: Wetland areas; near lakes, rivers, reservoirs, and coasts

Found throughout North America

1

2

3

4

5

6

NORTHERN CARDINAL

Cardinalis cardinalis

The northern cardinal is a songbird known for its song, performed by both males and females, and sharp head crest. The males are also known for their bright red feathers.

While the male cardinal has distinct red feathers and a black eye mask, the female cardinal has a paler, browner coloring.

The cardinal's wings are short and broad, allowing it to maneuver easily through its brushy habitat. Its strong, cone-shaped beak is great for opening nuts and seeds.

Order: Passeriformes
Family: Cardinalidae

Diet: Seeds, nuts, fruits, and insects

Size: 8 to 9 inches long

Habitat: Areas with plenty of shrubs and trees

Found throughout the eastern United States

1

2

3

4

5

6

BARN OWL

Tyto alba

The barn owl has small, dark eyes and a heart-shaped face. This adaptable bird makes its home in a building or hollow tree.

Barn owls make a range of noises, from screeches to hisses, but they do not "hoot" like other owls.

The coloring of a barn owl can include anything from white to gray or yellow to orange-brown.

Order: Strigiformes
Family: Tytonidae

Diet: Rodents, such as voles, mice, gophers, and shrews

Size: 15 inches long, less than 2 pounds

Habitat: Open areas, such as rough grasslands, marshes, and farming fields

Found throughout North America and on every continent except Antarctica

1

2

3

4

5

6

BLUE JAY

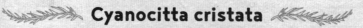

Cyanocitta cristata

This noisy forest bird has a pointed head crest, a black beak, and brilliant feathers of blue, white, and black.

Blue jays are social birds with tight family relationships. They are very vocal and even mimic sounds made by hawks.

Blue jay eggs can range from pale blue to light brown and spotted with brown or gray. Eggs take 17 to 18 days to hatch.

Order: Passeriformes
Family: Corvidae

Diet: Seeds, nuts, insects, and eggs

Size: 10 to 12 inches long

Habitat: Forest edges, particularly near oak trees

Found throughout eastern and central North America

1

2

3

4

5

WILD TURKEY

Meleagris gallopavo

The turkey is a large, plump bird with long legs and a long neck.
Males have a red *snood* (flap of skin over the beak) and
a red *wattle* (fleshy pouch under the neck).

Turkeys spend much of their days on the ground, but they sleep in trees at night for protection from predators.

Male turkeys are called "gobblers," and female turkeys are called "hens." Males have more extravagant feathers and puff them up to impress females.

Order: Galliformes
Family: Phasianidae

Diet: Mainly acorns, seeds, insects, and snails

Size: 50 inches long, up to 20 pounds

Habitat: Forests and wooded areas, as well as fields and clearings during the day

Found throughout the United States and Mexico

1

2

3

4

5

6

BALTIMORE ORIOLE

Icterus galbula

The official state bird of Maryland has a black head, black wings with white bars, and a bright orange underside.

The Baltimore oriole feeds on dark, ripe fruits. It pierces through the fruit's flesh with its beak closed, opens its beak, and then uses its tongue to lap up the resulting pocket of juice.

Orioles are excellent nest builders. Using twigs, grasses, hair, and other found materials, the female builds a nest that hangs from the end of a tree branch.

Order: Passeriformes
Family: Icteridae

Diet: Insects, fruit, and nectar

Size: About 7 to 8 inches long

Habitat: Gardens, forest edges, and open woodlands

Found throughout eastern North America

PILEATED WOODPECKER

❧ Dryocopus pileatus ❧

This woodpecker makes tapping sounds against wood in search of food. It has a black body, white head stripes, and a red crest of feathers.

Woodpeckers have long, strong bills and barbed tongues. These traits help them break through tree bark and pull out ants and beetle larvae.

The pileated woodpecker creates large holes in wood that later serve as nests for other animals, such as owls.

 Order: Piciformes
Family: Picidae

 Diet: Insects (including carpenter ants and beetle larvae), nuts, and fruits

 Size: Up to 19 inches long

 Habitat: Forests, including deciduous, coniferous, and mixed forests

Found throughout eastern and north-western areas of the United States and Canada

1

2

3

4

5

6

AMERICAN GOLDFINCH

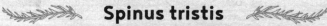

Spinus tristis

This small, cone-beaked finch has feathers that range from bright yellow to brown. It has black markings on the head, wings, and tail.

In summer, the male has bright yellow feathers. In winter, the feathers change to a light brown, which helps the bird blend into a less colorful environment.

The American goldfinch is a strict seed-eater. It may swallow an occasional insect, but only by accident!

Order: Passeriformes
Family: Fringillidae

Diet: Seeds

Size: About 5 inches long

Habitat: Open woodlands and floodplains to rural and urban areas

Found throughout North America

1

2

3

4

5

6

CEDAR WAXWING

Bombycilla cedrorum

The cedar waxwing is a fruit-eating bird with a crest, yellow underside, black eye mask, and boxy yellow- or orange-tipped tail.

The word "waxwing" refers to the tips of this bird's wings, which are coated in a shiny red material. Scientists still do not know the purpose of this wax-like feature!

It is rare to see just one cedar waxwing. This social bird is often seen in large flocks of 30 or more birds.

Order: Passeriformes
Family: Bombycillidae

Diet: Fruit and insects

Size: 5.5 to 7 inches long

Habitat: Open woodlands and forest edges

Found throughout North and Central America

1

2

3

4

5

6

GOLDEN EAGLE

 Aquila chrysaetos

This fast-flying raptor has a hooked beak, powerful talons, brown feathers, and golden coloring on its head and neck.

The golden eagle appears on the national flag of Mexico. It is the largest bird of prey in all of North America!

The average wingspan of a golden eagle is a whopping 7 feet! These fast birds can also dive at speeds of more than 150 miles per hour.

 Order: Accipitriformes
Family: Accipitridae

 Diet: Rodents, birds, fish, and other small- to medium-sized animals

Size: About 2.5 feet long, 6 to 15 pounds

 Habitat: Grasslands and mountainous zones with canyons and cliffs

Found in North America, Europe, Asia, and North Africa

1

2

3

4

5

6

RUBY-THROATED HUMMINGBIRD

Archilochus colubris

This bird has a long, thin beak designed to collect nectar from flowers. Despite its name, only the male ruby-throated hummingbird has a ruby-colored throat. The female has a dull white throat.

This hummingbirds doubles its weight when preparing for migration. It flies up to 20 hours straight to reach its winter home in Central America.

The ruby-throated hummingbird can beat its wings about 50 times per second!

 Order: Apodiformes
Family: Trochilidae

 Diet: Nectar, insects, and spiders

Size: 3.5 inches long

Habitat: Forests, fields and meadows, and orchards

Found throughout the eastern half of North America and into Central America

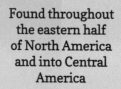

1

2

3

4

5

6

FASCINATING REPTILES & AMPHIBIANS

Herpetology is the study of reptiles and amphibians. When you're watching and recording information about these creatures, you are a naturalist and a herpetologist in training!

The green anole is a lizard and a reptile.

This amphibian is called a red eft, the juvenile phase of the red spotted newt.

Although reptiles and amphibians are cold-blooded animals that are often grouped together, they have some very important differences. At right, see which animals are reptiles and which are amphibians. Then learn about their main differences on the next page!

Reptiles	Amphibians
snakes	frogs
lizards	toads
turtles	salamanders
tortoises	newts
crocodiles	
alligators	

Then learn about their main differences on the next page!

Reptiles vs. Amphibians

How are they born?
Most reptiles lay their eggs on dry land. Reptile hatchlings emerge from the shells as miniature versions of the adults.

Most amphibians, however, lay their eggs in water or moist areas on land in large clumps that resemble jelly. In most species, the eggs hatch into tadpoles or larvae that look nothing like adults, and must go through drastic changes, called metamorphosis, into their adult forms.

How do they breathe?
Reptiles breathe through a pair of lungs. Amphibians, however, are born with gills. As they undergo metamorphosis, most amphibians develop lungs. But that's not all! Oxygen can also pass through an amphibian's skin. This process is called "cutaneous respiration." Some amphibians never develop lungs at all, relying solely on their skin to breathe!

Where do they live?
Reptiles have thick, scaly skin that allows some species to live in dry environments. The skin of most amphibians, however, is slippery and moist. These creatures must live in water or damp environments. Because reptiles and amphibians are cold-blooded, they are less active and harder to find in cold temperatures.

Watch out!
In North America, some reptiles you might encounter are venomous. Keep your distance from these animals, just in case!

American Green Tree Frog

IDENTIFYING REPTILES & AMPHIBIANS

Size

Can you guess the size of the animal in inches or feet? If not, compare it to an animal you know well. Is it bigger than a rabbit? Smaller than a mouse?

Shape

What is the animal's overall shape? Does it have a long body or long limbs? Is there any part of the animal that stands out, such as bulging eyes or a small head?

Color

What is the animal's main color? What other colors and patterns are present?

Desert Tortoise
Size & Shape: About 1 foot long with a domed shell. Front legs are large with big scales and claws.

Color: Tan and brown body and shell, which blend into the desert environment.

Garter Snake
Size & Shape: Long, thin body with a small head. About 2 feet long.

Color: Dark green body with light yellow "ribbons" that run from the head to the end of its tail. (Some garter snakes also have red stripes and checkered patterns.)

Northern Leopard Frog
Size & Shape: Slightly larger than a mouse, or about 4 inches long. Bulging eyes and thick, strong limbs.

Color: Brown and green with dark spots over the body and limbs. Light ridges along the back.

Habitat & Behavior

Location, habitat, and season are clues that can help you make an educated guess as to what species you're seeing. If you're on the Pacific Coast or in southeastern parts of the United States, the frog you see is probably not a northern leopard frog. If you're in a lush meadow, you are probably not looking at a desert tortoise.

What is the animal doing? Is it resting in the sun or looking for food? How is the animal moving its body?

Desert Tortoise

Habitat: Seen year-round in the deserts of the southwestern United States. Lives in burrows when temperatures are very hot or very cold.

Behavior: Moves slowly and eats vegetation in the desert scrub. Uses strong, sharp claws to dig burrows in the ground.

Is it making a noise, such as a croak or a chirp? Any other interesting characteristics?

Northern Leopard Frog

Habitat: Lives in marshes, ponds, and wet meadows and grasslands. Present in the United States and Canada.

Behavior: Spends most of its time in or near water. Quick jumper. Hunts insects, worms, and smaller frogs.

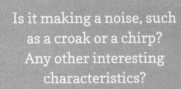

Garter Snake

Habitat: Found throughout the continental United States, in Mexico, and in southern areas of Canada.

Behavior: Active during the day. In colder climates, it hibernates in the winter.

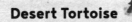

COMMON BOX TURTLE

Terrapene carolina

The box turtle has a large shell made of fused bones covered with thick bony plates called "scutes." It can pull its head and limbs completely within its shell!

Box turtle eggs and babies are prey for many animals. However, the high-domed shell of the adult box turtle makes it too difficult for most predators to consume.

There are six *Terrapene carolina* subspecies, each with widely varying color patterns in the shells.

Order: Testudines
Family: Emydidae

Diet: Fungi, plants, slugs, snails, and earthworms

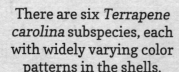
Size: 4 to 9 inches long

Habitat: On moist ground in open forests and along the edges of wetlands

Found throughout eastern North America

1

2

3

4

5

6

7

GILA MONSTER

Heloderma suspectum

This large, colorful venomous lizard hibernates in the winter and stays cool during summer in an underground burrow. It is most often seen in the spring in the morning and late afternoon.

This is one of the few venomous lizards, so be careful if you see one. If you are too close and it feels threatened, it may deliver an extremely painful bite.

The gila monster can eat up to half its own body weight in one sitting! It stores fat from these big meals in its tail, which allows it to go months between feedings.

 Order: Squamata
Family: Helodermatidae

 Diet: Mainly bird and reptile eggs, but also small birds, mammals, frogs, lizards, and insects

 Size: About 2 feet long

 Habitat: Deserts and arid scrublands, especially in rocky areas

Found in the southwestern United States and northern Mexico

1

2

3

4

5

6

PACIFIC TREE FROG

Pseudacris regilla

This frog is green and brown and has large, bulging eyes. It has long digits and limbs that are great for climbing, but despite its name, it is usually found on the ground or in low vegetation.

The tree frog's skin ranges from light yellow-green to dark olive. Some frogs will slowly change colors and patterns when the seasons change, to help them blend in with their environments.

The body of a tree frog may be wet and slippery, but it has sticky pads on the ends of its toes to help it climb.

Order: Anura
Family: Hylidae

Diet: Insects

Size: Up to 2 inches long

Habitat: Forests, grasslands, and among plants around wetlands, such as marshes, wet woodlands, and ponds

Found in western areas of the United States

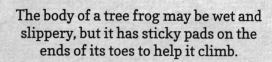

1

2

4

3

5

6

7

RED SALAMANDER

Pseudotriton ruber

This salamander has no lungs. It can be orange-brown to a bright red color, and the older it gets, the darker its spots become.

The red salamander is a nocturnal amphibian, which means most of its waking hours are at night. During the day, it can be found tucked away under rocks, logs, leaf litter, or other coverings.

The red salamander is one of the lungless salamanders. It absorbs oxygen from the air and water through its skin and the lining of its mouth.

Order: Caudata
Family: Plethodontidae

Diet: Insects, spiders, worms, and smaller salamanders

Size: 4 to 6 inches long

Habitat: Small streams and moist woodland environments. Both aquatic and terrestrial

Found throughout the eastern United States

1

2

3

4

5

6

AMERICAN GREEN ANOLE

Anolis carolinensis

Also called "the Carolina anole" (pronounced ah-no-lee), this sleek lizard has a tapered tail that is longer than the rest of its body!

It can change its skin color in response to its environment. It is bright green when active, but might turn brown if cold or stressed.

The male has a pink, textured throat fan called a "dewlap," which it inflates to impress females and claim territory. The female has a simple white throat.

 Order: Squamata
Family: Dactyloidae

 Diet: Insects, spiders, and other invertebrates

 Size: Up to 7 inches long

 Habitat: Upland forests, scrublands, swamps, and fields

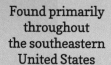

Found primarily throughout the southeastern United States

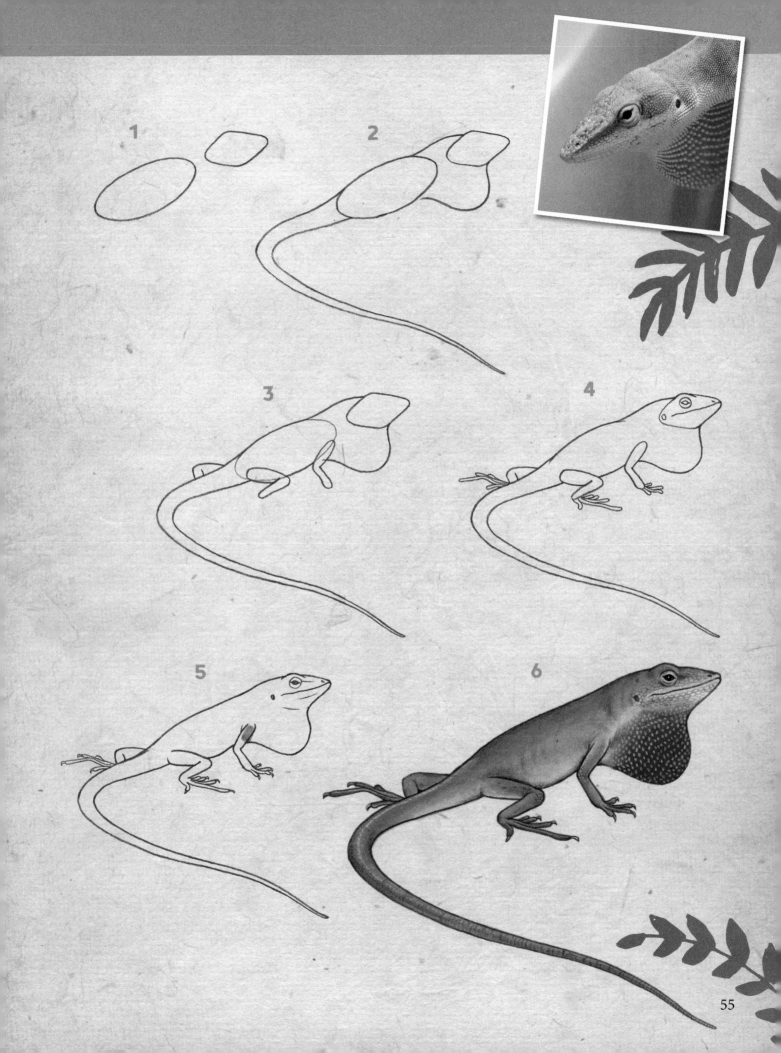

1

2

3

4

5

6

ALLIGATOR

Alligator mississippiensis

The alligator is a large reptile with four short limbs, a long snout, sharp teeth, tough skin, and a flat, powerful tail.

How do you tell the difference between a crocodile and an alligator? An alligator has a wider snout that hides most of its teeth when its mouth is closed.

The skin of an alligator's back contains hard, bony plates, which protect the alligator's organs from harm.

Order: Crocodylia
Family: Alligatoridae

Diet: Fish, small mammals, and birds

Size: 10 to 12 feet long, up to 1,000 pounds

Habitat: Freshwater rivers, lakes, swamps, and marshes

Found in coastal areas of the southeastern United States.

1

2

3

4

5

Keep far away from this animal! The alligator is a very dangerous predator. If you see one in the wild, view from a distance with an adult.

6

INCREDIBLE INSECTS

Entomology is the study of insects. When you're watching and recording information about these critters, you are a naturalist and an entomologist in training!

Leafcutter bee

Woolly bear caterpillar, which turns into the Isabella tiger moth

Known as the "mother of entomology," Maria Sibylla Merian (1647–1717) is famous for her discoveries regarding the butterfly's fascinating life cycle. She was also a skilled artist who created detailed drawings and paintings of the insects and plants she studied.

Insect Basics

What are insects?

Insects have six legs, two antennae, a body made up of three segments, and an exoskeleton (or a hard outer shell instead of internal bones and a spine). Many insects also have wings.

How many are there?

Insects make up the largest group of living organisms on the planet. There are about 1 million described species of insects, and scientists estimate that there are millions more not yet discovered!

What are the main groups of insects?

The four largest orders of animals under the class Insecta include Coleoptera (beetles), Diptera (flies), Lepidoptera (butterflies and moths), and Hymenoptera (ants, bees, and wasps). There are more than 360,000 beetle species on Earth—more than any other type of insect!

Monarch butterfly

Are they insects?

Is a spider an insect? No! A spider has eight legs, two body segments, and no antennae. Is a centipede an insect? No! A centipede has too many legs and body segments. Is a housefly an insect? Yes! It has wings, antennae, and three body segments.

IDENTIFYING INSECTS

Size

Compare an unfamiliar insect with one you know well. Is it bigger than a fly? Smaller than a butterfly? Low-to-the-ground like an ant?

Shape

What is the insect's overall shape? Does it have big, visible wings? Does it have compound eyes? Long legs?

Color

What are the insect's main colors? Are they bright to warn predators, or do they blend into the environment?

Blue Dasher Dragonfly

Size & Shape: About the size of a smaller moth, about 1.5 inches long. Long, skinny body tapers toward the "tail."

Color: Males are mostly blue. Females are yellow and brown.

Buffalo Treehopper

Size & Shape: Tall, thin body with a sharp point above the head.

Color: Mostly green to match the surrounding leaves.

Ladybug

Size & Shape: Small with a rounded body.

Color: A shiny red outer shell with black spots, a black head, and black legs.

Habitat & Behavior

Think about where you are, what kind of habitat you're in, and what season it is. For example, if you're hiking in the Rocky Mountains, the dragonfly you see is probably not a blue dasher. If there are no trees or bushes around, the insect you see is probably not a treehopper.

What is the insect doing? Is it in a tree or on the ground? Is it still or active? Does it fly, jump, or crawl?

Blue Dasher Dragonfly

Habitat: Found near still water, such as lakes, ponds, and marshes. Lives in Mexico, the United States, and southern parts of Canada; avoids dry, high-altitude areas, such as the Rocky Mountains.

Behavior: The male spends much of its time near the water's edge, whereas the female typically stays among vegetation.

Is the insect making a noise? Does it have any characteristics not yet mentioned?

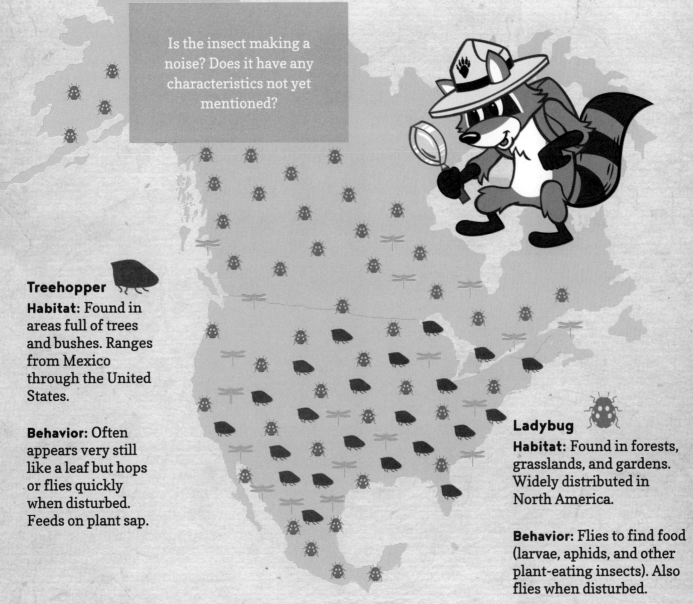

Treehopper

Habitat: Found in areas full of trees and bushes. Ranges from Mexico through the United States.

Behavior: Often appears very still like a leaf but hops or flies quickly when disturbed. Feeds on plant sap.

Ladybug

Habitat: Found in forests, grasslands, and gardens. Widely distributed in North America.

Behavior: Flies to find food (larvae, aphids, and other plant-eating insects). Also flies when disturbed.

MONARCH BUTTERFLY

Danaus plexippus

The monarch is known for its bright orange, black, and white coloring. This butterfly migrates every year and can travel thousands of miles!

The easy-to-spot monarch butterfly does not need to blend into its environment. Its bright appearance warns predators that it is poisonous and unpleasant in taste!

The monarch migrates south to Mexico for the winter. When spring arrives, a new generation flies north. Monarchs west of the Rocky Mountains migrate to the Southern California coast for the winter.

Order: Lepidoptera
Family: Nymphalidae

Diet: Nectar; the caterpillar's host plant (where it lives and eats) is milkweed

Size: 3.5 to 4 inches wide

Habitat: Meadows, open fields, and gardens with milkweed

Found throughout the United States and in Mexico

1

2

3

4

5

STINK BUG

Family: Pentatomidae

The stink bug has a triangular body and a shell-like back. It is named for the foul smell it produces to ward off predators. There are many species of stink bugs that come in different colors and sizes.

The stink bug is not technically a bug. That name is reserved for the true bug order, Hemiptera, members of which have needle-like sucking mouth parts to drink plant juices, body fluids of other insects, and even blood.

Some stink bug species are considered pests (like the non-native marmorated stink bug shown below), but many are considered beneficial insects.

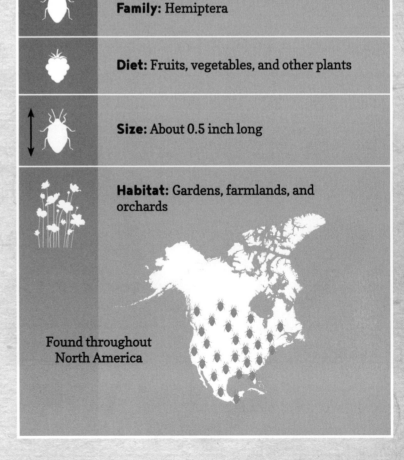

Class: Insecta
Family: Hemiptera

Diet: Fruits, vegetables, and other plants

Size: About 0.5 inch long

Habitat: Gardens, farmlands, and orchards

Found throughout North America

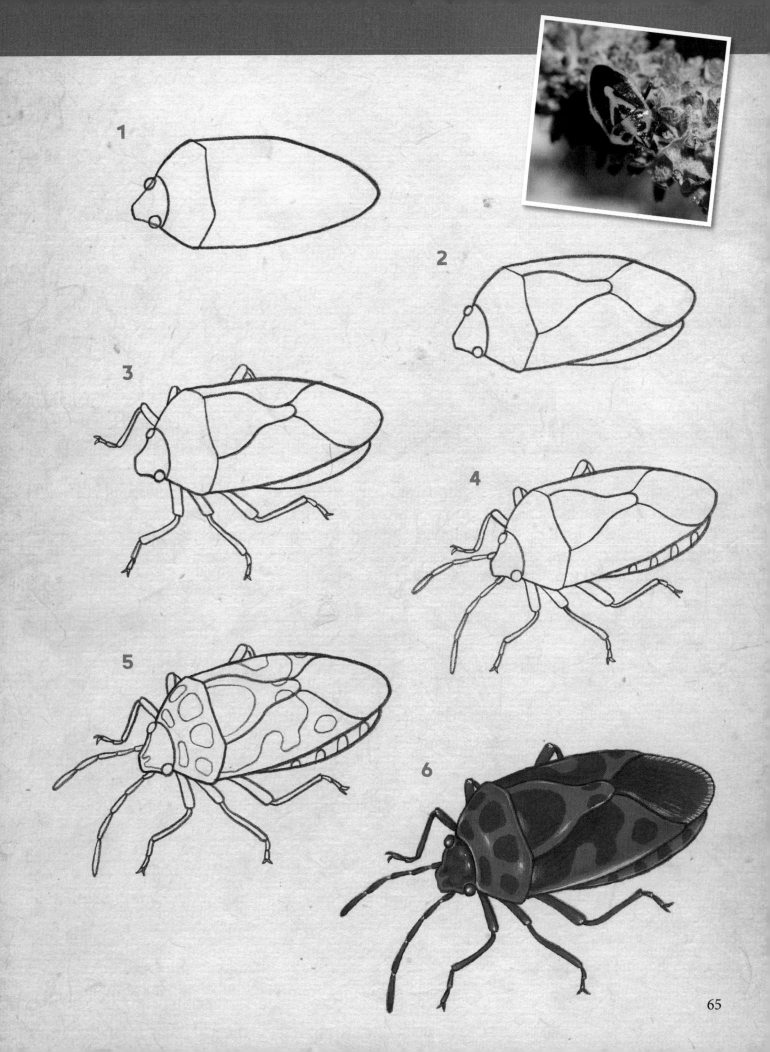

1

2

3

4

5

6

CRICKET

 Genus: Gryllus

The cricket has strong hind legs for jumping and is best known for its chirping sound. There are many species of different sizes, shapes, colors, and behaviors.

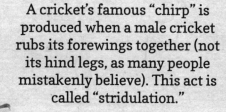

A cricket's famous "chirp" is produced when a male cricket rubs its forewings together (not its hind legs, as many people mistakenly believe). This act is called "stridulation."

Crickets chirp faster as the temperature increases.

Order: Orthoptera
Family: Gryllidae

Diet: Small insects, larvae, rotting plant matter, flowers, fruit, grasses, and seedlings

Size: 0.12 to 2 inches long

Habitat: A variety of environments, including fields, meadows, and wooded areas

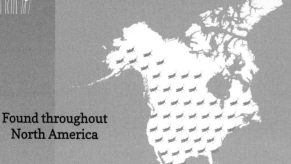

Found throughout North America

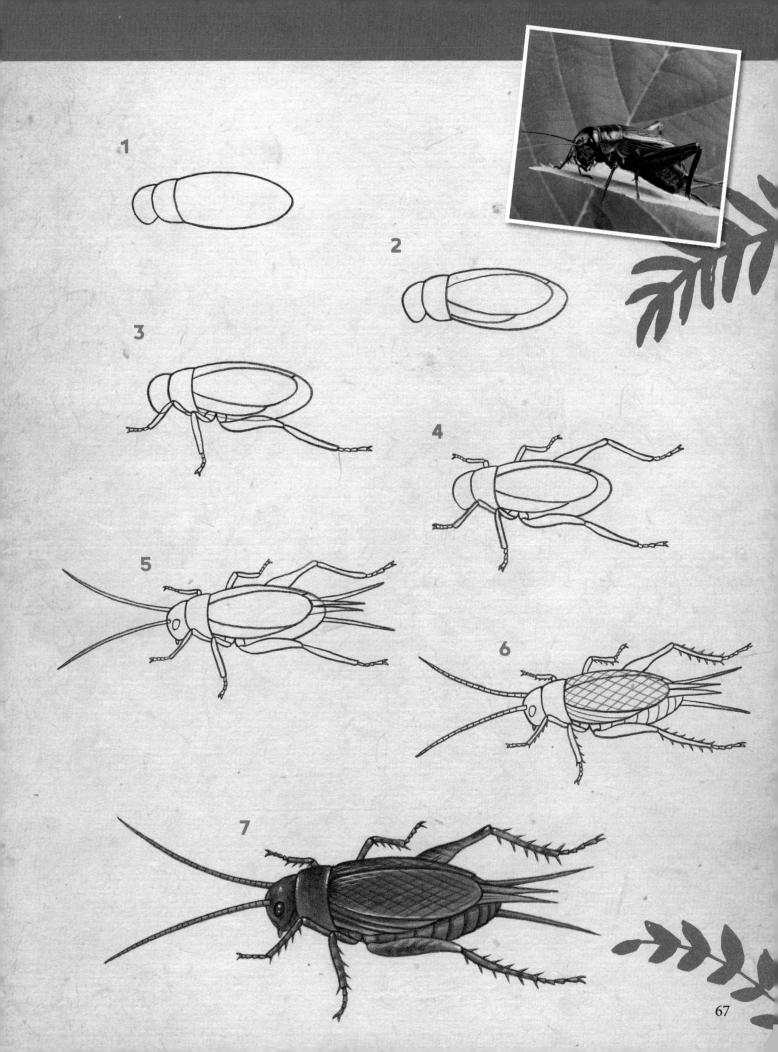

1

2

3

4

5

6

7

RED-BANDED HAIRSTREAK

 Calycopis cecrops

This gray butterfly has a red streak with fine black and white lines on the underside of each wing. Its legs and antennae have black and white bands.

The caterpillar of this butterfly feeds on the fallen leaves of sumac, wax myrtle, and oak trees.

The red-banded hairstreak has small tails and eyespots that create the illusion of a head on its backside. This feature protects its actual head from being attacked by predatory spiders.

 Order: Lepidoptera
Family: Lycaenidae

 Diet: Nectar; the caterpillar lives on and eats the leaves of sumac, wax myrtle, and oak trees

 Size: About 1 inch wide

 Habitat: Overgrown fields and forest edges

Found in the southeastern United States

68

1

2

3

4

5

6

WALKING STICK

Diapheromera femorata

This slender insect disguises itself among plants and trees. Its coloring and spiny, ridged body provide excellent camouflage, making it look just like a stick!

The walking stick's eggs are also camouflaged. They look like seeds!

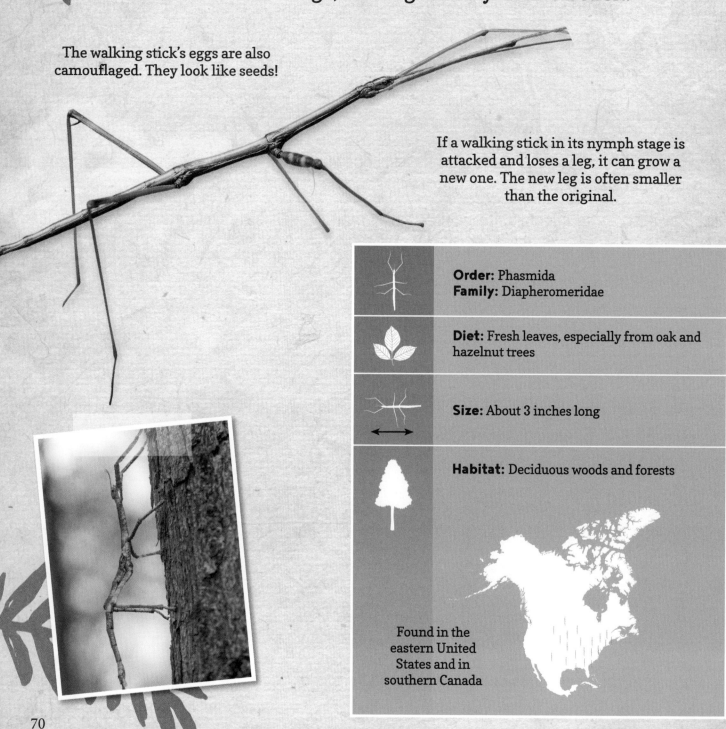

If a walking stick in its nymph stage is attacked and loses a leg, it can grow a new one. The new leg is often smaller than the original.

Order: Phasmida
Family: Diapheromeridae

Diet: Fresh leaves, especially from oak and hazelnut trees

Size: About 3 inches long

Habitat: Deciduous woods and forests

Found in the eastern United States and in southern Canada

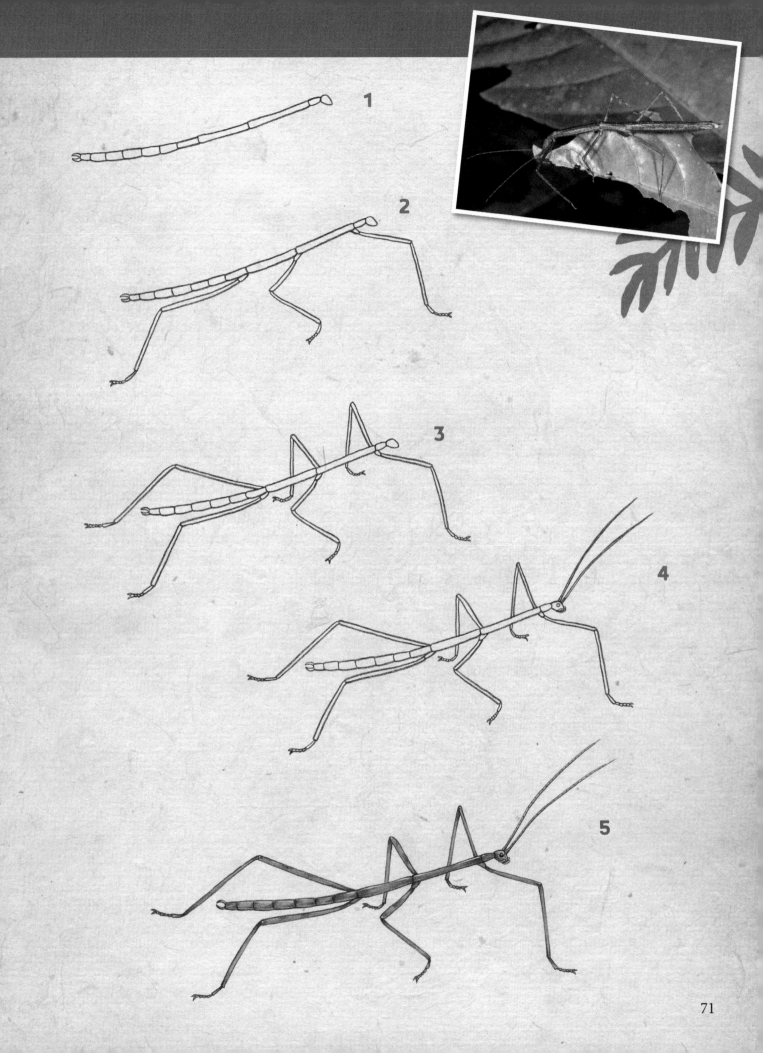

17-YEAR CICADA

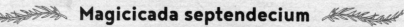

Magicicada septendecium

The 17-year cicada has reddish-orange eyes and legs, and clear wings with orange veins. There are a few different kinds of cicadas, but this is the largest.

The 17-year cicada gets its name from its fascinating life cycle. Just once every 17 years, these long-lived insects, which live underground during their juvenile nymph stage, come out as adults to mate. For about two months, the males can be heard "singing" to attract the females.

Because all 17-year cicadas mate at once in a short period of time, there are a lot of cicadas during this time, up to 1.5 million cicadas an acre. And they're very loud!

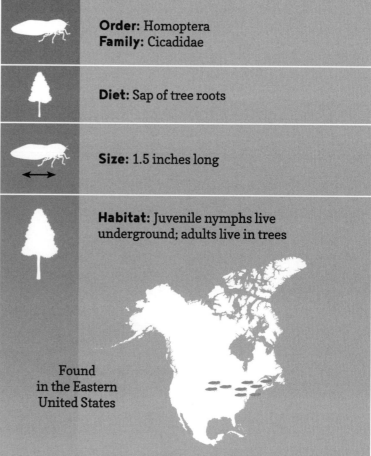

Order: Homoptera
Family: Cicadidae

Diet: Sap of tree roots

Size: 1.5 inches long

Habitat: Juvenile nymphs live underground; adults live in trees

Found in the Eastern United States

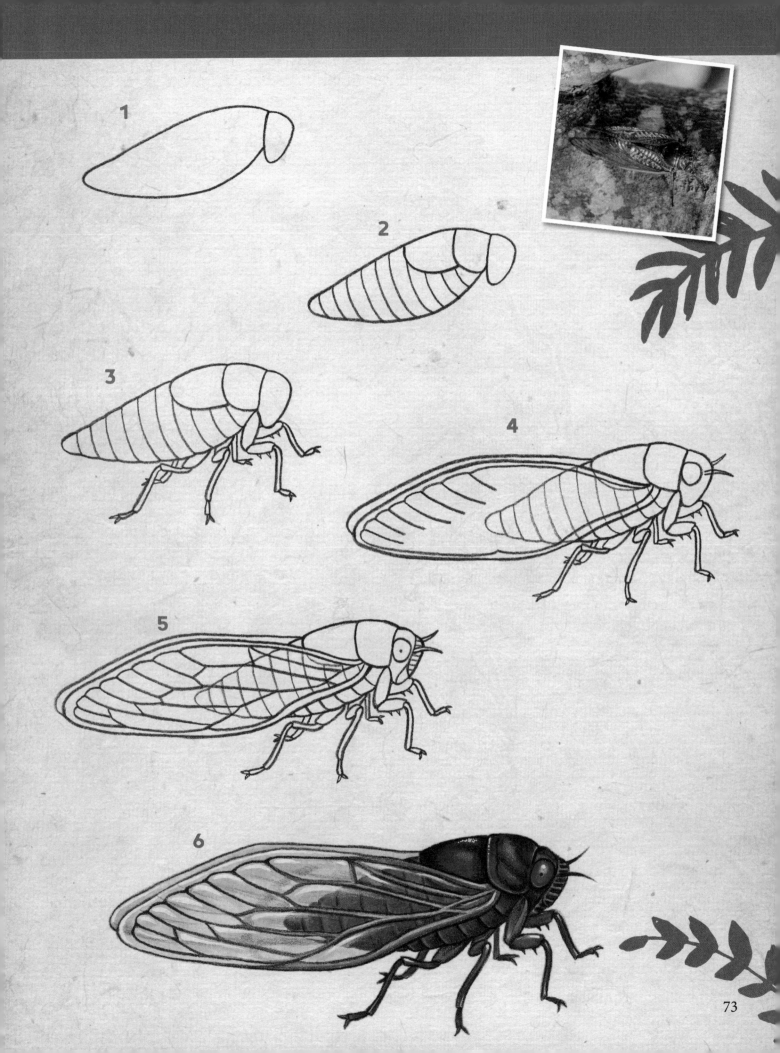

1

2

3

4

5

6

LUNA MOTH

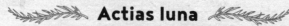

⚘ Actias luna ⚘

This moth has a large, green body with broad, long-tailed wings. It gets its name from the moon-like eye spots on its wings. The male moth also sports feathered antennae!

The luna moth does not eat! As a caterpillar, it feeds on tree leaves, but once it emerges from the cocoon, it doesn't have a complete mouth. It got enough energy from the food it ate as a caterpillar to mate and reproduce, which is the only goal of an adult luna moth.

The luna moth has a very long tail that helps protect it from bats. These predators are drawn to attacking this area instead of more important areas, such as the head and abdomen.

 Order: Lepidoptera
Family: Saturniidae

 Diet: Tree leaves, such as walnut, hickory, and birch (as a caterpillar)

 Size: About 4.5 inches wide

 Habitat: Deciduous hardwood forests

Found throughout eastern North America

1

2

3

4

5

6

7

YELLOW JACKET

The yellow jacket wasp is a winged insect with a black-and-yellow coloring. There are several species of wasp grouped together as "yellow jackets."

While some people are afraid of the yellow jacket because it can sting repeatedly (unlike bees), this insect is actually very beneficial for humans. It eats many plant pests that kill crops of food that people eat.

Some wasps are solitary, but the yellow jacket lives in a colony and builds a nest underground. A colony can contain thousands of workers!

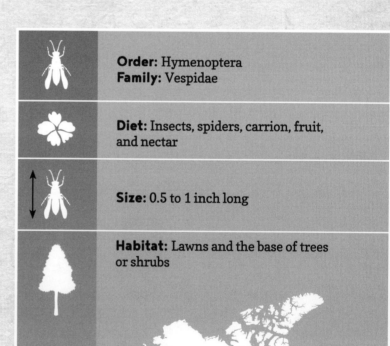

Order: Hymenoptera
Family: Vespidae

Diet: Insects, spiders, carrion, fruit, and nectar

Size: 0.5 to 1 inch long

Habitat: Lawns and the base of trees or shrubs

Found throughout North America

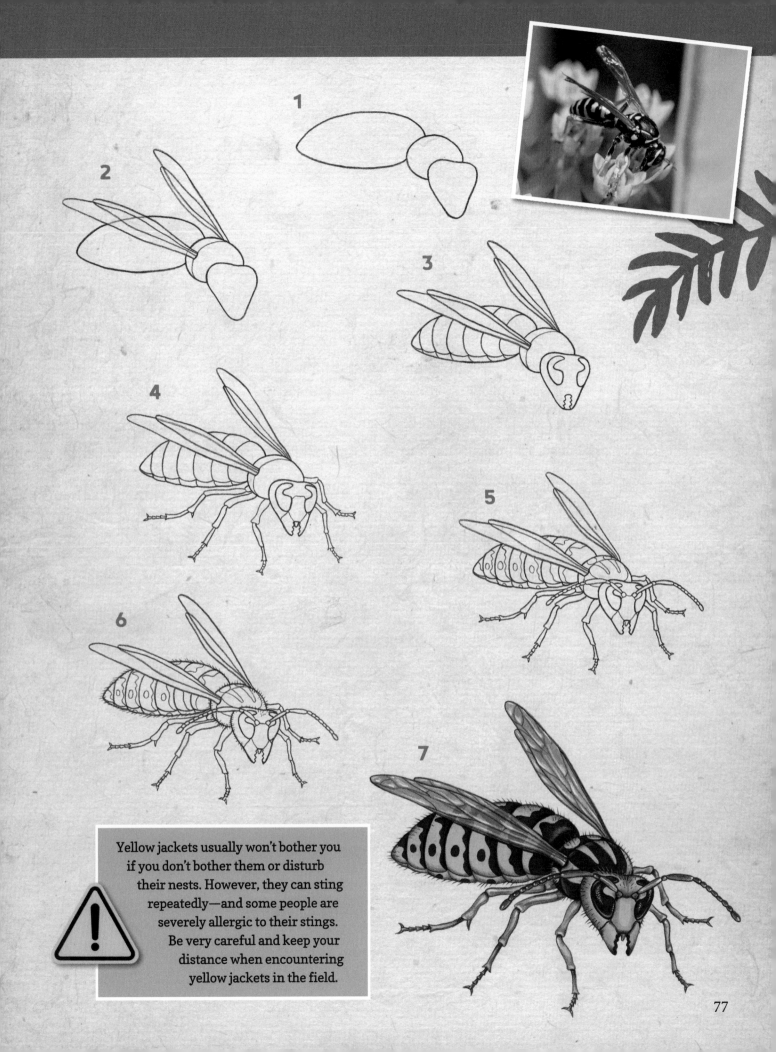

1

2

3

4

5

6

7

Yellow jackets usually won't bother you if you don't bother them or disturb their nests. However, they can sting repeatedly—and some people are severely allergic to their stings. Be very careful and keep your distance when encountering yellow jackets in the field.

RED ADMIRAL BUTTERFLY

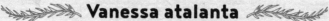

Vanessa atalanta

This brownish-black butterfly has red-orange bands and white and blue markings on its wings. It is one of the most widespread butterflies on earth!

The caterpillar lives on and eats stinging nettle. But don't touch stinging nettle without gloves! This plant is protected by stinging hairs on its stems and the undersides of its leaves.

This butterfly migrates or hibernates in the winter, but it tolerates pretty cold weather for a butterfly. It can be seen flying around on sunny winter days.

 Order: Lepidoptera
Family: Nymphalidae

 Diet: Rotting fruit, sap, bird droppings, and nectar; the caterpillar's host plant is stinging nettle

 Size: 3 inches wide

 Habitat: Moist woodlands and fields, from the subtropics to the tundra

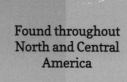

Found throughout North and Central America

CONTINUE THE ADVENTURE!

Now that you've gotten to know some of North America's fascinating animals, don't stop learning! There are endless birds, reptiles, amphibians, and insects to seek and study. Besides looking in your own backyard, go to local parks and hiking trails. Make a list of all the nature preserves, animal sanctuaries, and national parks that you'd like to visit. You'll be surprised at how many resources await you!

Eastern Bluebirds

About the National Wildlife Federation

Securing the future of wildlife through education and action since 1936, the National Wildlife Federation is one of America's largest conservation organizations. In January 1967, the National Wildlife Federation started publishing *Ranger Rick®* magazine, which has cultivated generations of young wildlife enthusiasts to become lifelong partners in protecting our environment alongside their charismatic ambassador, Ranger Rick, and his friends.

Read more Ranger Rick! Check out the *Ranger Rick*, *Ranger Rick Jr.*, and *Ranger Rick Cub* magazines at RangerRick.com.

And get these other guides from Ranger Rick:

National Wildlife Federation Naturalist
David Mizejewski is a naturalist, author, and the host of NatGeo WILD's television series *Pet Talk*. As a wildlife expert, he has appeared on many television and radio shows, including *Conan*, *Good Morning America*, and the *Today* show. A lifelong naturalist, David spent his youth exploring the woods, fields, and wetlands, observing and learning all about the natural world around us. He lives in Washington, D.C.